Super Special Sister
Copyright © 2022 by Brittany Murray-Bradford
ISBN Print Book: 978-1-0880-3679-2
All rights reserved.

No part of this book may be used or reproduced by any means, graphic, electronic, or mechanical, including photocopying, recording, taping, or by information storage retrieval system without the publisher's written permission except in the case of brief quotation embodied in critical articles and reviews.

This book is dedicated
to my dear friend Christy.
To Mary-Elizabeth Robinson
and her daughter Kimar and Family.
To Tabitha Parks and her daughter Jojo.
To the Apple Employee with Verizon Wireless,
thank you for the information.
To all of the people, families & friends
that inspired me to write this book.

This is my twin sister.

My sister is S
Special.

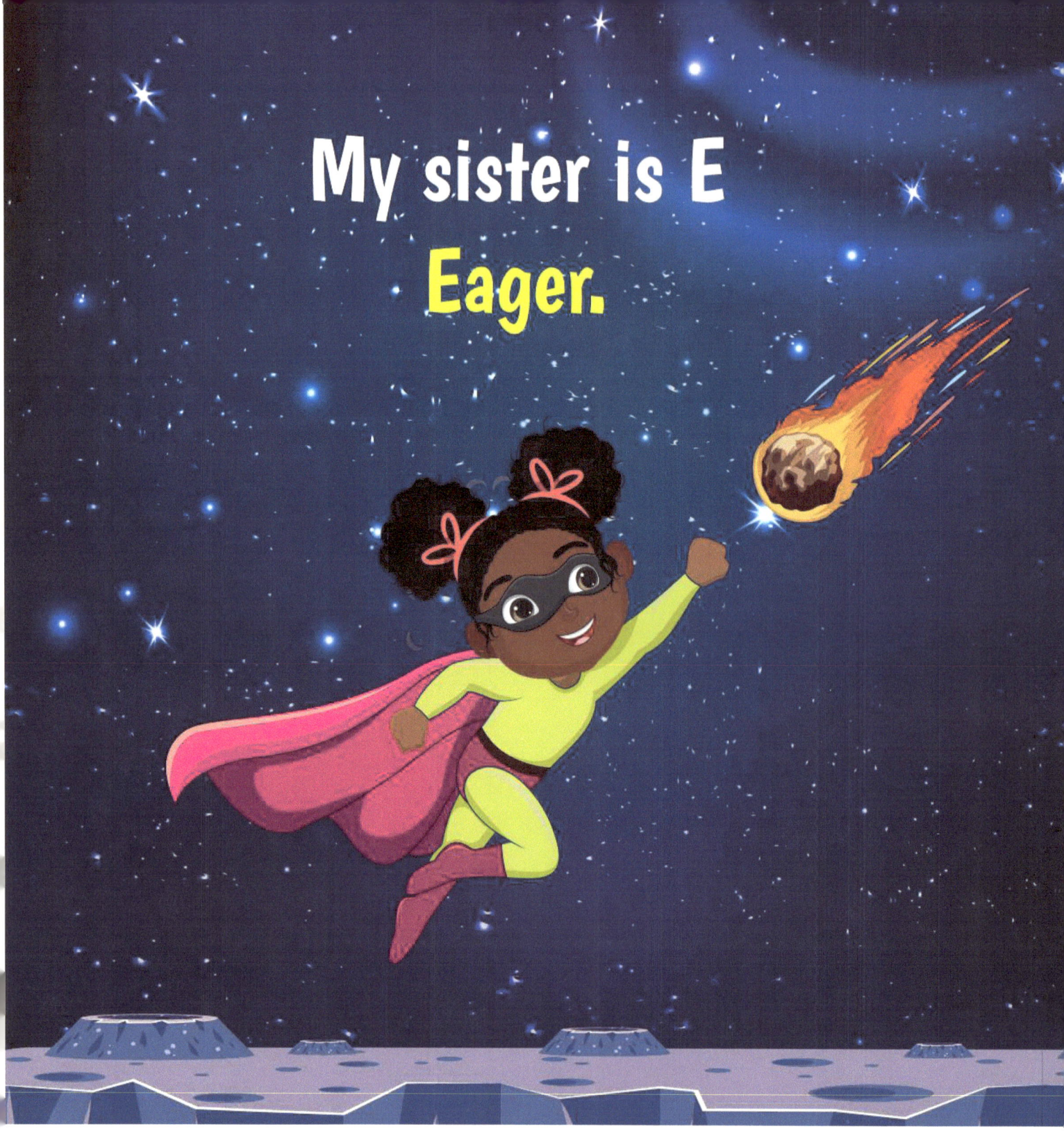

My sister is E
Eager.

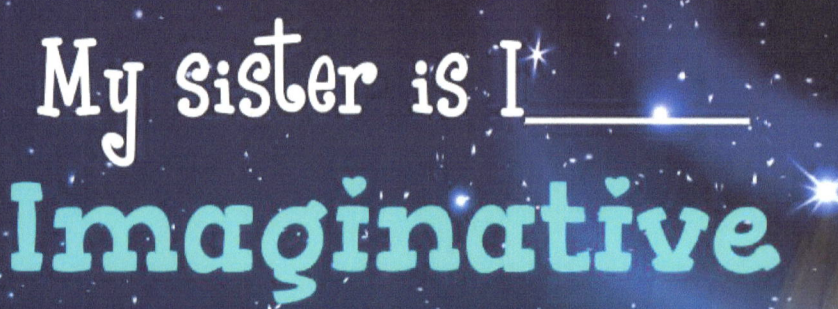

My sister is I____

Imaginative

My sister is A Awesome.

WOW... She is very SPECIAL!

Yes and there are many more special people just like her all around the world.

God created us in His image and likeness. So even though we are different He loves us all the same.

Brittany Murray-Bradford was blessed to grow up in a Christian household where her parents were married, high school sweethearts. The oldest of three siblings, she attended public school and grew up in a small town in Pasadena, Maryland, just outside of Baltimore, Maryland. It is located near Washington, D.C., and Virginia. This area is commonly referred to as the DMV. Growing up in this area provided an appreciation for rural and urban living—her collegiate education in Upstate New York. Upon graduating with a Bachelor of Science in Nursing, she moved back to Maryland to work as a Registered Nurse. After marriage, she and her husband dedicated much of our time to professional development, church participation, and community service pursuits domestic to abroad. It was small things in life that they began to seek to impact a positive outcome. She is the proud mother of two precious sons.

www.ingramcontent.com/pod-product-compliance
Lightning Source LLC
Chambersburg PA
CBHW041439010526
44118CB00002B/130